Up Home

RABBIT HOUSE PRESS
Versailles, KY 40383

Published in the United States of America by Rabbit House Press, October 2023.

For inquiries about author appearances and/or volume orders contact us at rabbithousepress.com.

ISBN: 979-8-9871928-8-7 (Hardcover)
ISBN: 979-8-9907833-4-8 (Paperback)

Editor: Erin Chandler
Cover and interior design; formatting: Brooke Lee

Chapter one photo spread; photos pgs. 62, 72, 80 & 81: Bob Rouse
Chapter one, page 13 photo: Mary Beth Rouse
Chapter eight photo: Steele Rouse
Hermosa flower image by Harryarts on Freepik

Unless otherwise noted, all images are from the Amy Parrish Rouse Perry collection, used with permission.

Up Home

A Family, a Tragedy, &
the Holly Hill Inn

Bob Rouse

RABBIT
HOUSE
PRESS

rabbithousepress.com

*To my great-uncle Jim Parrish.
It was the story of his death that gave
birth to this book.*

CONTENTS

ACKNOWLEDGMENTS

I'm grateful to my sisters, Kay and Amy, whose minds I tapped for memories of our old relatives when, it could be argued, we are now old relatives ourselves. Amy's collection of family photos, records, and writings form the backbone of this book, and Kay's unearthing of a taped interview with Honeywood was as insightful as it was timely.

I'm also grateful to my wife, Mary Beth, who was forced to read one essay after another. As always, she provided solid, sensible advice.

I must thank the team at Rabbit House Press—specifically Erin Chandler, Brooke Lee, and Emily Wilhoit. They embraced my eagerness to tell the stories of my Parrish family and the house called "up home," and they provided me the freedom (with guardrails) to do it.

And then there are the subjects of this book. Some I knew and adored; others I never met. But each life connects with mine. The love they had for family and place is part of me…now and forever.

The three Parrish siblings, circa 1907. Left to right: Honeywood, Katherine (Nat), and—with curls—Jim.

Introduction

People & Places

A family history comprises generations of people and various places they inhabited. One such place helps define my people—at least one branch of my family tree.

For a century, Hermosa was owned by members of the Parrish family, sons and daughters who came to Midway, Kentucky, before it was either Midway or Kentucky.

My sisters and I are the eighth generation of Parrishes in Midway, starting with James, who arrived in Kentucky in 1781. And I can't say that my Parrish forebears were especially extraordinary, because every family who came to Kentucky long ago has a story to tell—filled with success and sadness, with simplicity and complexities.

I can't say that Hermosa, now the Holly Hill Inn, is the finest mansion in the Bluegrass, but it is exceptional. Starting in 1903, it was the home of Ike and Desdemona Parrish and their children—Honeywood, Nat, and Jim—and decades later, I grew up right next door. Two of the three helped shape my life, and the third left a tragic imprint on our family that cannot be erased. Hermosa, the formal name given to the house, was never used. To the family it was always just "up home."

These people and this place are part of me, and I gladly introduce them to you. And maybe you knew them...or people like them. We can celebrate their joys and mourn their sorrows, and we can share their hearts. Their past is our today, passed to us either through DNA or TLC.

Honey, Nat, and Jim lived lives that differed in length but grew from the same family, the same place...up home.

The Parrish children—Jim, Nat, and Honeywood—aboard Jasper, "a fat, lazy, broad-backed Shetland pony," circa 1910

Chapter One

Thanksgiving in July

The Holly Hill Inn has been the scene of a million meals: romantic dinners, festive gatherings, business meetings, and wedding receptions. I've enjoyed those events at the Holly Hill Inn, but the meal there that means the most to me is an annual family tradition: Thanksgiving in July. My sisters and our families don't gather on the fourth Thursday in November, so we celebrate—and give thanks— during the summer at the Holly Hill Inn, once known as Hermosa.

My family goes back a ways with the hefty house atop Cogartown Hill in Midway, Kentucky. My great-grandparents, Isaac and Desdemona Parrish, bought the house in 1903, and there they raised their three children, Honeywood, Katherine (called Nat), and Jim.

When "Mr. Ike" and "Mama Des" purchased the house, they named it Hermosa after the wild English rose they found growing in the garden. And while the thorns might have stuck, the name didn't, as Honeywood described in a journal she began writing at age eighty-six. "For some reason, we never used 'Hermosa,'" she wrote. "It was just 'our home' or 'up home.'"

A hundred years before it was the Parrish home, and even before the town of Midway was founded, the property belonged to Thomas Stevenson. It rested on the southeast corner of Stevenson's Crossroad and contained Stevenson's Tavern, a large stone and brick structure built circa 1800. On February 8, 1832, it was established as the area's first post office, and serving as the first postmaster was—you guessed it—Mr. Stevenson.

In 1839, Stevenson sold the tavern and land for sixty dollars an acre to Hancock W. Davis, who soon thereafter watched his investment burn down. A few years later, in the early 1840s, Davis built the first sections of what is now the Holly Hill Inn. He incorporated some doors and windows, and possibly walls and fireplaces, from the earlier building.

Mr. Davis built three rooms facing Leestown Road (now U.S. 421): the present-day kitchen, dining room, and front entry hall. The main entrance would have been on the north side of the house and not where it is today.

Davis lived in the building until 1854, when he sold it to Squire William A. Moore for seventy dollars an acre. Moore was a local magistrate and president of the Midway Paper Mill Company. He and his wife, Mary, added some Victorian touches to the house. A room was also added to each side of the parlor/entry hall, and the main entrance to the house was moved to face the current North Winter Street.

After the squire died, Mary remained in the house until 1903, when it was sold to my great-grandparents. Mr. Ike and Mama Des undertook a major remodeling. The Parrishes added plumbing, electrical wiring, two bathrooms, a furnace, new hardwood floors, a side porch, and a large Colonial Revival-style veranda. The wooden front door was replaced by a half-glass door, still in use today, to bring light into the dark entry hall.

They chose a concrete surface for the porch, rather than wood boards, so the children could roller skate there. (I've heard this story so many times, I would expect my ancestors to have formed a roller derby team. The porch originally featured wood railings, which would have led to spectacular flips during a match.)

The porches of this house got a lot of use, especially during the summer. In addition to skating, the front porch was also used by the Parrish family as an after-dinner retreat from the hot house. And the side porch, where the bar is now located, was used for less formal meals. Above it was a screened-in sleeping porch, where family members and houseguests alike bedded down on steamy nights.

After the move to Hermosa, Mr. Ike and Mama Des retained their large tobacco farm but used the immediate grounds of Hermosa for the family's needs. The ten-acre property included a large garden yielding corn, tomatoes, green beans, and other produce; two grape arbors for jelly, juice, and wine; and fruit trees: apple, pear, and cherry.

Today, in addition to the inn, you'll see a couple of private homes on the property. One of them is the house I grew up in. My dad (Ike Rouse, Honeywood's son) and mom (Jean) built our home next door to Hermosa in 1955, three years before I appeared. The other house, closer to the Holly Hill inn, belongs to Ouita and Chris Michel, the owner of the Inn and a portfolio of other restaurants, including one in Lexington named Honeywood.

A century ago, you would have seen a bigger collection of buildings: a cabin where the household help lived, two chicken houses, a pigeon house (squab was a favorite meal), a smoke house for curing hams, a barn that housed mules and milk cows, a buggy house (later heated when automobiles sputtered into existence), a shop filled with tools, and, in the cellar beneath it, an ice house.

I remember only the cabin, which I was certain was haunted, and the shop/ice house combo. Located just northeast of the main house's kitchen, the shop looked like a small barn. Two large sections of the wood floor were hinged doors, opening up to a cellar where big blocks of ice, cut from nearby ponds, were stocked in the winter and used later to preserve food and provide a chill to summertime tea. After the electric refrigerator was invented, the ice house was converted into a mushroom cellar.

As I understand it, Desdemona was the fiscal leader of the family. Tall and slender with light brown hair and eyes, it was Mama Des who managed the garden/orchard/poultry/dairy/mushroom operation, oversaw the family's finances, and even handled the 1935 purchase of a cottage in Naples, Florida.

Mr. Ike was a capable farmer and, as described by Honeywood, "a careful dresser." He was an amiable man noted for his hospitality, according to my father, who lived with his parents in Midway proper but spent many nights—weeks, even—with his grandparents. At Hermosa, the table leaves were kept in the large dining room table to accommodate the many visitors, expected or unexpected.

"My grandfather never met a person who didn't become a dear friend, and most of them were brought home to dinner," my dad once said. "They practically ran a restaurant over there."

Most of the meals at Hermosa were prepared and served by hired help. A cook would prepare platters of food and deposit them in a sort of closet that connected the kitchen and dining room. In the dining room, a server would open a door on the other side of the closet, retrieve the platters, and serve the guests at a formal table adorned with china, silver settings, and a white linen tablecloth.

As a kid, I never tired of hiding in the service window or using it to crawl between the kitchen and dining room. It was the closest thing I had to a secret passageway. Besides Mr. Ike's "dear friends" joining the family for meals, there were other visitors at Hermosa. Like many Midway families, the Parrishes often housed local schoolteachers. Nat hosted her friends here, too, and their names alone speak of a bygone time: Agnes, Juliet Lee, and Ida Kenney.

The girls would ride horses, climb trees, and of course, roller-skate on the porch. Another frequent visitor was James Cogar, a family friend who later served as the first curator of Colonial Williamsburg and directed the restoration of nearby Shakertown.

To add to the mealtime comings and goings, Hermosa was headquarters for Nat and Honeywood's brother, Jim, and his buddies, many of whom lived on Cogartown Hill. Long before the field across the driveway was an overflow parking area, it was a baseball field populated by neighborhood sluggers. When baseball was impractical, the boys would gather in the front hall of Hermosa, where Mr. Ike had set up a pool table for Jim and his friends.

Nat stayed at Hermosa for her whole life. After she died, my dad and Honeywood inherited it. No longer Hermosa but not yet the Holly Hill Inn, the house was home for several years to cousin Jim Rouse and his growing family. They, like the couple who followed them as renters, called it "Nat's house," which seemed only fitting to me.

***

During my early teen-age years, my mother was stricken with empty nest syndrome when my oldest sister, Kay, left Kentucky for college in 1972. This affliction puzzled my other sister, Amy, and me, as we were still in the nest. Mom needed a project to battle her malady, and she decided to create a classy, comfortable bed-and-breakfast.

At the time, there was no fine dining in Midway and no rooms for rent. Mom scouted several Midway houses; each required too much renovation to meet accessibility requirements. Why Mom had not considered Hermosa from the beginning, I don't know, but she eventually viewed the house with new eyes and targeted it for a makeover.

In creating the Holly Hill Inn, Mom had to make loads of decisions, and the best one she made was to hire Rex and Rose Lyons as innkeepers. They were diligence and creativity personified. Honeywood, too, knew a good team when she saw one. "Rex runs the Inn and Rose runs Rex," was how she summed it up in her journal.

Converting a country home into a country inn was an enormous task, though. Because of a 1977 fire at a Kentucky nightclub, new public facilities of any size had to meet the same safety requirements of a major hotel. Mom and Dad and the Lyonses encountered stringent regulations calling for an electrical upgrade here, a fire escape there, and a handicapped-accessible bathroom or two around the corner. "Code" became a dirty word at the Holly Hill Inn.

When the establishment opened in 1979, the Lyonses lived in three rooms above the dining room and kitchen, and the two front rooms upstairs were guest rooms, sharing a comically small bathroom off the hall. The downstairs room on the southwest corner was also designated as a guest room; it adjoined a bathroom that was later removed to provide more space on the side porch.

As the inn caught on with visitors and locals alike, Honeywood reflected in her journal on the new function of her old home. She must have been asked—or wondered herself—how the rest of the Parrish family would view the changes to a repurposed Hermosa.

"I think Mama and Nat would love the house's transformation and thoroughly approve," she wrote. "But Daddy wouldn't like it—[in his mind] it was already perfect!"

For many couples, the Holly Hill Inn became the perfect place to celebrate a wedding, often accommodating three events per weekend. In our time, both of my sisters and I dragged our newly pronounced spouses to the inn for our receptions. Ideally suited for a party—roomy and intimate at the same time—the inn held special meaning for the three of us: We were up home.

Mom died in 1991, and the Lyonses carried on her dream of a small-town inn for another decade. It was not Dad's dream, though, and he talked to me one day about selling the inn. From a financial standpoint, the risk of keeping up with an aging building did not outweigh the modest rental income. As part-owner, along with Dad and my sister Kay, I slowly digested the notion of parting with Nat's house.

About a week after that conversation, I was at a Lexington restaurant called Emmett's, another rambling home that had been converted into a dinner house. An occasional writer for a local magazine, I was profiling Emmett's and its popular chef, Ouita Michel. As she toured my wife and me through the building, she showed us the upstairs rooms. Our conversation went like this:

"These are former bedrooms that we use for seating groups," Ouita explained.

"I'm familiar with the concept," I said. "I grew up near the Holly Hill Inn."

"Oh, I *love* the Holly Hill Inn," Ouita gushed. "I would love to own it one day."

Now, I'm no real estate genius, but I know a willing buyer when I see one melting in front of me.

We never placed an ad; we never sought another bid. In one short on-site meeting, we worked out what stayed with the inn and what moved out. Nat's piano moved to my house.

Once again, Nat's house was reconditioned, this time by the Michels. The kitchen in particular was re-energized, as it received updated electricity, plumbing, lighting, flooring, and space. A walk-through butler's pantry, situated between the dining room and kitchen, was removed. The service window—my secret passageway—was sealed up.

My father, Ike, donning a chef's coat and hat for a 2010 photo on the front porch of Holly Hill Inn with his favorite chef and neighbor, Ouita Michel

Throughout the house, floors were refinished, walls and ceilings were rejuvenated, and rooms were redecorated. Years of use were cleaned from banisters and chandeliers, and new carpets, chairs, fixtures, and wine cabinets were hauled in. The Holly Hill Inn greeted the new day under new ownership.

And the rest, as they say, is history—but not really. Why do they even say that? History has already happened. History is Stevenson's Tavern, Squire Moore and his widow, and Hermosa. The rest of this story is the tale that Chris, Ouita, and daughter Willa will tell as they move forward.

My dad, whose middle name is Parrish, once said that the Michels represent the perfect blend of host and entrepreneur to occupy his forebears' home.

"Nat would have liked the people and the fun times.... My grandmother would have liked the bottom line."

For my family, the bottom line is the ideal arrangement the Holly Hill Inn provides us. We still enjoy this house—its old memories and its new meals—while someone else worries about the roof, the plumbing, and the corn pudding. We gather "up home" as a family every year for dinner in midsummer, when we're all in Kentucky. That's our Thanksgiving in July.

Three siblings, 2023: Bob Rouse, Amy Rouse Perry, Kay Rouse Lark (seated)

Jim Parrish, Centre College yearbook photo, probably 1927

Chapter Two

Young Jim Parrish

"Everybody loved young Jim Parrish," it said in the *Blue Grass Clipper* on August 11, 1932. Everybody might have loved an old Jim Parrish, too, but we'll never know. James Ware Parrish III drowned while swimming in Elkhorn Creek near Midway, Kentucky. He was twenty-seven.

I dearly loved Jim Parrish's sisters: my grandmother Honeywood and my great-aunt Katherine (Nat). Both of them lived their lives, from start to finish, in Midway. Honey and Nat were educated women, fascinating and fun, and they treasured their family. It killed a part of them when their brother died. And it killed the family line, too: Jim was the last Parrish male.

Jim's drowning began as a Friday afternoon swim with Honeywood, her friend Clara MacLemore, Whitsitt Wallace, and Clara's nephew John Stone. The party had driven the mile and a half from the Parrish home (now the Holly Hill Inn) to Moore's Mill, which sat beside Elkhorn Creek. Below a dam that powered the mill was a pool that was a popular spot for swimming. Although the *Clipper* article doesn't mention them, two children—Ike Rouse (my dad) and Clara's daughter, Lily May—were also among the swimmers, but they were whisked away before details of the drowning were recorded.

It's confounding that Jim would drown. He was not just a strong swimmer, but a heroic one, too. In an editorial in the same issue of the *Clipper* that carried the page-one news of Jim's death, J.W. Reigner described an episode from four years before, when Jim and a cousin were driving across the bridge at Moore's Mill and heard the cries of a woman: "My God...save my children!"

Reigner wrote that Jim and his cousin leapt from their car and sprinted to the creek—undressing as they ran—jumped in and rescued two young girls "who were drowning when they had come up for the last time."

And describing yet another amazing coincidence, Reigner went on to say that on the day before Jim drowned, "near the very spot where he lost his life," he rescued "little Benny Roach from a watery grave."

Jim was an accomplished athlete in the water and on land. He played baseball and football at Midway High School and later at Centre College. During warm months, Midway boys played ball in the Parrish's side yard, which was a perpetual baseball diamond. The gang also gathered indoors.

"Daddy had a pool table set up in the downstairs front hall, and all of Jim's friends were welcome at any time," Honeywood wrote in her journal, many years later.

By all accounts Jim was as pleasant a guy as you'd ever want to know.

"He was nice and friendly—not loud—and popular with the girls," Lily May recalled in late 2017. "Fairly tall with auburn hair."

A Delta Kappa Epsilon fraternity brother wrote this about Jim in the Centre College yearbook in 1927, his senior year: "Jim will not soon be forgotten by those fortunate enough to have known him. Always cool, apparently taking his time about everything, he has made a success in the classroom, on the diamond and wherever else he happened to be."

Jim was the manager of the Centre football team and accompanied the team on road trips, including one to New York City in 1925. The '27 yearbook contains a line about his role. "Jim Parrish did himself proud. He watched the college's money as he would guard his life, and not a stray dollar eluded his watchful eyes."

What Jim did not see that day at Moore's Mill was a chunk of wood—or perhaps a stone—that swept over the dam and struck him on the side of his head, opening a hole in his skull and knocking him unconscious.

When the other swimmers noticed that Jim was not among them, they assumed he was behind the waterfall, hidden from view on a ledge of the dam. Not finding her brother there, Honeywood and the others frantically looked along the creek banks and swam around in the creek, which was swollen from recent rains.

Whitsitt drove to town and ran inside the general store owned by his brother, Top. "Ropes!" he shouted. "We need ropes to drag the creek at Moore's Mill."

News spread quickly in the small town, and dozens of people sped to the scene. "Everybody in Midway who had an automobile rushed there," said the *Clipper*.

Jim's father, Ike, was there, along with James Ware Parrish II, who was Jim's uncle (after whom he was named). No fewer than four Midway doctors were there, too: Anderson, Risque and Voigt, as well as

Jim Parrish, about 16, with the Parrish's smokehouse in the background

Dr. B.F. Parrish, also Ike's brother, who had retired from practice.

A half-hour after the search had begun, John Stone, standing in shoulder-high water some fifteen feet from the dam, felt a body bump against him underwater. With help from Whitsitt, the visitor from Ohio dragged Jim to the shore; Mr. Ike met them there.

A rescue unit from the Lexington Fire Department arrived on the scene eight minutes after being summoned, and for more than an hour the firemen used a Pulmoter to force air into Jim's lungs. Despite their heroic efforts, and despite the assistance of the four hometown physicians, Jim Parrish never drew another breath.

Mr. Ike "was taken away from the scene," according to the *Clipper's* account. "The father went all to pieces to see his only son lying there, cold in death."

Ike's brother, the elder James Parrish, was also overcome with grief. "It was more than he could stand. He broke down and had to be led to his automobile by Dr. Voigt."

Those men were not the only family members and friends who suffered.

"Giving up Jim by drowning in the summer of '32 was such a blow to us; it looked as if Mama couldn't accept it. And Nat really never did. Jim was only 27 years old," Honeywood wrote in her journal. She went on to explain that the Parrish name ended with the early deaths of not only her brother, but also a cousin, who had died at college more than a decade before Jim drowned.

"Uncle Ben lost his only son, Tom, at Princeton. He was 19 years old," she wrote. "Two old brothers losing only sons."

On the day of Jim's funeral, the communal grief was profound. A brief funeral was conducted at the Parrish home, where Jim's body laid in a gray casket, which was covered with flowers. The body was then taken to the Lexington Cemetery and followed by a long line of cars. Jim's Midway friends and Centre College fraternity brothers served as pallbearers. His mother was so overcome with grief, she was unable to go to the cemetery. And according to the *Clipper*, even the funeral officiants struggled, including R.S. Wilson, the former minister of Midway Christian Church who had baptized Jim.

"Rev. Wilson was to commit the body to the grave, but he broke down and had to be led away," the newspaper account said.

On that Monday morning, the people of Midway buried a young man with a bright future. At the time of his death, Jim was an agent for the American Tobacco Company. Prior to that, he had served for a time as principal of the Midway school.

"He was, in every way, a noble and splendid young man," Reigner wrote in his editorial, titled, "The Tragic Death of James Ware Parrish."

"Of attractive personality, of marked ability, of affable disposition, of polished manners and of sturdy and stalwart manhood, it is so sad that he had to die before his work had hardly begun."

With time, the people of Midway recovered, and the town went on to mourn the deaths and celebrate the lives of other friends and relatives.

But Jim's family—his mom and dad and Honeywood and Nat—were never quite whole again. On that hot, heart-breaking day in August, their lives were robbed of a shining light, a kind soul.

Decades later, my sister Amy and I were helping our mom move furniture out of the old Parrish home, and Amy discovered a small box in the back of a drawer. It was packed with curly auburn hair. When Amy revealed the contents, Mom said, "Don't let Honeywood see this."

The sight of her brother's hair, probably from his first haircut, would have been too painful—nearly 50 years after he drowned.

What would Jim have done with his life? What people would have been affected by his actions and words? What difference would he have made?

I live with my family on Moores Mill Road, and I routinely cross the same bridge Jim was crossing when he abandoned his car to save two drowning children. Beneath it runs the Elkhorn Creek, where the old mill dam used to stand…and where Midway kids used to swim.

Born a quarter of a century after Jim died, I never knew my great-uncle nor the children—my cousins—he never had. I would have spent time at his house; my family would have shared holiday meals with his. I would have learned things from him and, perhaps, followed his example.

On the face of it, I suffer the loss of Jim Parrish, too. It's possible I would be a different, better person for having known Jim and benefitted from his strength of character.

But maybe I have. Maybe many of us have.

That boy Jim rescued, "little Benny," grew up to be Dr. Ben Roach, described as a "medical legend in Kentucky" by a University of Kentucky president. Ben Roach co-founded the UK Markey Cancer Center, he established the Family Practice department at UK, and he founded the nursing program at what is now Midway University. Dr. Ben maintained a family practice in Midway for fifty-five years, and he treated and delivered countless residents, including me.

By all accounts, Jim was a kind and capable guy who made friends easily, and it's fair to assume he was a significant influence on his companions in Midway and at Centre College. It's certain that Jim made an immeasurable impact on his sisters, Honeywood and Nat, and they, in turn, encouraged, amused, and inspired me. I never met the man, but I have to think he's part of me…part of Midway.

"Everybody loved young Jim Parrish," you know. And I would have loved an old one.

Jim Parrish, circa 1924

A rare photo of Nat, taken around 1913 in the side yard of her home.

Chapter Three

Nat in a New Light

I was crying as hard as a twelve-year-old kid can cry. My great-aunt Katherine, known by all as Nat, had died. My folks allowed me to attend her funeral, but I bet they were wishing they had instead dropped me off at Eastern State Hospital in the care of a psychiatric nurse. I don't remember anything about the service, only that I was crying uncontrollably in the Milward and Sons limousine that carried Nat's closest family members to the cemetery.

We were close, for sure. Nat lived right next door, as my parents built our house on the property that included the Parrish family home, then called Hermosa and now known as the Holly Hill Inn. Nat was a year old when her parents—my great-grandparents Ike and

Desdemona Parrish—bought the place, and she lived the rest of her life there.

For her last six years, she lived alone. Up until 1964, Nat resided in the big house with her mother; Nat's father had died 20 years before. In a journal that my grandmother Honeywood kept, she wrote that no one but her—and the cook, Siretha—knew "the extent of Nat's faithfulness and unselfish devotion" in caring for their mother.

Nat also cared for the family home. Honeywood wrote that one winter when her parents went to Florida, Nat "stayed home and hand-scraped and refinished all the cherry woodwork in Hermosa. This was a tremendous job, which she did all alone except for a farm helper who helped her scrape...only a very few times."

I wasn't yet alive to help with that chore, but during my growing-up years I visited next door regularly, often in the morning. There's a picture of me sitting outside at Nat's house, wearing my pajamas and slippers and scraping icing from a pan.

I remember that whenever my family would go on a trip, Nat would give my sisters and me a bag of small presents to unwrap at certain times during the drive. And Nat gave me my first driving lesson, right there in the side yard. I was only five or so and relied on her to push the pedals. Sitting on Nat's lap, I could steer her '62 Dodge Dart past the sundial and flower garden, whip a U around the grape arbor, and bump up onto the driveway. And I could even shift gears; the Dodge featured a push-button transmission. My sister Kay recalls that one of us kids (not me) was driving Nat's car out on the farm and ran into a fence.

Nat herself was known to have some questionable driving habits. Long after her death, Midway folks would talk of how Nat, an avid reader, would often drive through Midway with her right hand on the steering wheel and her left hand holding the book she was reading.

Nat was an accomplished musician—a graduate of the Louisville Conservatory of Music—who gave piano lessons to local pupils. She entertained at family gatherings and also played the organ at Midway Presbyterian Church. One tale told often in our family was that Nat overslept one Sunday, and, with no time to dress, she threw a three-quarter-length mink coat over her nightgown, got to church on time, and played in front of the congregation, from prelude to postlude, wearing that mink.

And while Nat enjoyed playing at church, she apparently thought the audience didn't always pay attention to her performance. To test her suspicion one Sunday, she played a solemn and grandiose rendition of "Yes, We Have No Bananas" as the postlude. Another time she morphed a Bach fugue into a regal

"Happy Birthday to You." These stories still survive, so I guess the congregation really did notice.

Quirkiness was a hallmark of Nat's personality. In her 1999 book, *A Soul Remembering*, longtime Midway resident Jonelle Fisher shares examples of Nat's behavior that helped make her such a beloved Midway personality. Back in Nat's day, most Midway residents didn't lock their doors, and when Nat would call on a friend and no one answered her knock, she would walk on in and, to let the neighbor know she had come calling, Nat would take a chair in the front hall and turn it upside down.

Another one of Nat's habits described by Jo Fisher sounds like a good idea to me. Before embarking on a trip, Nat would buy, stamp, and address postcards to her friends (and us, I suppose), and she'd write on each one that she was having a grand time on vacation. Then, somewhere in the middle of her trip, she'd drop the postcards in the mail.

At home in her big house, Nat would climb out her bedroom window to sunbathe on the porch roof when she felt like it. She taught us how to say "I love you" you in French and German. And whenever we spent the night there, we'd each find a little present under our pillow.

Mrs. Fisher concludes her portrayal of my great-aunt with these heartfelt words: "Funny things were part of who Nat was, but it was not the best part. She was generous and kind to a fault, and understanding. I never heard her say a bad word about another human being. She truly made a difference in all of us with her life."

Nat was regarded as a beautiful woman by everyone who knew her…unless they were put off by her facial deformity. Nat had orofacial clefts, birth defects that affected her speech and distorted her upper lip. As she dressed in a costume each year and spooked the children at the Midway School's Halloween Festival, so also did Nat also scare away potential suitors with her everyday appearance.

Nat in a school photo in front of the Midway Public School, circa 1912. In the first row of girls, she's third from the left (and she likely marred the image of her face)

There are only a few photos of Nat. She shied away from cameras or looked down when a photo was snapped. But I never heard Nat complain about her looks or lament her spinsterhood. Of course, if she expressed those sorrows to anyone, it wouldn't have been to a little boy. What Nat did share with me, though, was a zest for life and a spirit of love.

It's been more than half a century since my crying jag at Nat's funeral, and except for my grandmother's journal and Mrs. Fisher's book, I've had no new information that adds to my knowledge about my great-aunt, and nothing that helps me understand who she was…until recently.

My sister Amy shared with me a poem that Nat wrote to a distant cousin on a birthday or at a pivotal time in her life. While I don't know the details of why it was sent, I fully understand why it was written. I have, in the past few years, discovered the curative power of poetry, and I can imagine that Nat found comfort in expressing her thoughts—revelations, really. They were, perhaps, sentiments that had weighed on her, and with this outward expression, her words must have helped her to better see herself, her life, and her future.

Here's the poem; I have tweaked its line breaks a bit to enhance readability.

This is the age I had not cared to reach:
This outer edge of youth, when here and there
A strange new silver thread slips in the hair,
And careless days grow farther back
With each additional birthday.
These have been the years I dreaded secretly.
But suddenly I find it is a lovely age,
And I was blind to beauty that must follow
When the ears are more attuned to listening,
The touch more sensitive,
And eyes have learned at last to see detail
And not go hurrying past to newness always.
This age is much more satisfying,
Now that the heart has lately found
Love's not in taking...
But in giving greatly.

Handwritten at the bottom of the typed, untitled poem is this note from Nat:

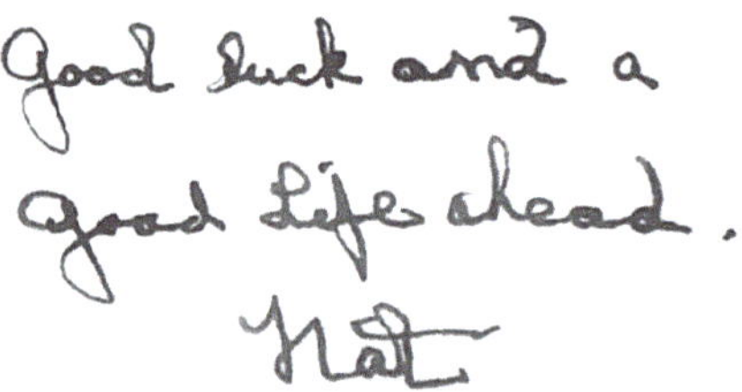

The poem reveals a layer of Nat I had neither known nor imagined…a depth of thought and insight that was not part of my funny, huggy memories.

But now I see Nat in a new light. Now I have proof of the kind soul her friends knew. And now I feel her in my own life…again.

Nat's Dodge Dart at Hermosa, circa 1964

Nat, in front of the family's cottage in Naples, Florida, holding a pompano she caught, 1950s

Honeywood with Howard in 1922, the year they wed, with Jim on the front porch of Hermosa

Chapter Four

Honey's Houses

The Happiest of Homes

My grandmother Honeywood Parrish Rouse was as unique as her given name…and as sweet as the name my sisters and I called her: Honey.

She was born in 1898 in a house on the family farm in northern Woodford County. Within a couple of years, she and her family moved a half-mile south to the house they named Hermosa.

"But for some reason we never used the name," Honey wrote in her journal. "It was just our home or 'up home.'"

In that journal, Honeywood writes about her home and family—parents Ike and Desdemona, brother Jim, and sister Nat—and the life they lived in the early 1900s.

"My father was not affluent like Uncle Jim and Uncle Ben," she wrote. "But nobody could have had a happier home, or as much fun as the Ike Parrishes!"

When I think of Honey, I hear her melodic voice. Not in song, but in word. In the course of everyday speaking, Honey's elocution ranged from high trills to low rumbles and every note in between.

My sister Kay recently unearthed a tape of an interview she conducted with our grandmother in 1982, when Honey was eighty-four. I was struck by Honey's decidedly Southern accent; I guess I had forgotten how much a daughter of the South she was.

She pronounced "hair" with two syllables: HAY-uh. And "door" was DOH-wuh. On the tape, Honey spoke of Midway neighbors who were also somehow related (hey, it's a small town). She made several references to a cousin, Lucy Rumley, as "Cud'n Lucy."

Honey's sweet voice was an accompaniment to a full life. Though she traveled widely, Honey lived her entire life in Midway, close to family and friends. Nearly everything I know about her years at Hermosa I learned from her journal. But by the time I was born, Honeywood had been out of that home for almost four decades. In my mind, Hermosa was Nat's house, and Honey will forever be linked to two other homes: one in Midway, a mile from

Hermosa, and another in Naples, Florida, a thousand miles away. They, too, were the happiest of homes.

Pinkerton Place

Similar to Washington, D.C., Midway has a white house that's home to the president. In our case, it's the president of Midway University, who lives in a two-story Greek Revival house on the corner of Winter and Stephens streets. The brick exterior has been painted white since the late 1940s.

Before it was the president's home, it was, for 46 years, Honey's house. Honeywood married Howard Rouse in 1922, and their first home in Midway was the "Little Brown House," also on Winter Street. They lived there for two decades, raising one son— my dad, Ike—after losing another one to meningitis at the age of six.

In 1944, Howard and Honeywood bought Pinkerton Place, the big house up the street from their brown bungalow. It was owned by "Cud'n Lucy," who watched with horror as my grandparents made extensive changes to the interior and exterior. They were restoring the home, built a century before, to its original style. It had been, Honey wrote in her journal, "badly Victorianized." After Howard took out a large, square newel post at the bottom of the staircase and replaced it with a curved volute, Cousin Lucy declared it the final blow and never entered the house again.

As a kid, I would have appreciated the big newel post to better stop my slides down the banister. The final curve always threw me off, literally.

Along with my sisters, Kay and Amy, I spent many a Friday night at Honey and Howard's house. Honey would read us bedtime stories, usually falling asleep and awakened by our giggles and nudges. I remember absolutely nothing from those books. I won't forget the lovely voice that read them, though.

I well remember the Saturday breakfasts that Honey fixed us. I rarely think of her as a great cook, mostly because she employed a talented woman, Juanita Darneal, to prepare evening supper and Sunday dinner. But Honeywood's breakfasts were her own creation: eggs and bacon with fried grits cakes, and every now and then she'd serve a real treat: fried fish—bluegill or crappie, maybe trout—that Howard had caught in the farm pond the night before.

The memory of those small, delicious filets coated with crumbly cornmeal makes me want to grab a pole and head to the pond right now.

Sunday dinner was a big deal. After church, our family would join Honey and Howard and her sister—my great-aunt Nat—at either Pinkerton Place

Top: Pinkerton Place (now called Pinkerton-Rouse Place).
Bottom: Hermosa. Both houses are on Midway's Winter Street.

or Hermosa. (We didn't actually use those names, of course…just Honey's or Nat's.)

Howard always told some good stories, but we'd also get a laugh whenever Honey, sitting at the head of the table closest to her kitchen, would summon Juanita for the next course by pressing with her foot a button beneath the rug that sounded a buzzer in the kitchen…except Honey seldom found the buzzer on her first attempt. We'd see her rocking slightly and hear the thuds of misplaced stomps, and we'd know more food was on the way—maybe.

Honey's house was elegant but not pretentious. Formal but fun. And Honey could really entertain.

I remember a Christmas party with a houseful of Honey and Howard's friends and neighbors. The highlight for us kids was finding a present Honey had hidden for each of us. It was a real treasure hunt. Each child at the party had a small card with his or her name on it, tied to a piece of yarn and dangling from the landing on the staircase. From that landing, we reeled in our card and then followed the string of yarn on a tortuous trail through the upstairs rooms— under beds and around chairs and dressers—until we arrived at the gift Honey picked for us.

It's possible that Honey devised that hunt only one time, but it's as strong as any early memory I have of her house.

As I grew older, I came to appreciate Honey's house for its strategic location. My buddies and I would "camp out" in a secluded section of the backyard, providing us with a staging area to roam the streets of Midway, staying out way later than our parents would have allowed. And when I started dating a girl who lived next door, Honey's house reached a new level of importance.

Howard died in 1974, and on that morning he failed to wake up, Honey called our house. "Howard's gone," she cried into the phone. My mom and dad were out of town, and the girls were away at college, so I went downtown to help. Honey had also called Jim Rouse, my cousin and an attorney, and he was there to supervise things.

I remember Honey being on a solemn mission to determine exactly when Howard had suffered his first heart attack, probably a decade earlier. I can only guess that Honey had helped Howard eat healthier and worked to make his life more comfortable. Maybe his survival for all those years was a point of pride for Honey.

I was sixteen in 1974, and Honey lived another sixteen years in her big, wonderful home. She had housekeeping help, but she took care to keep Howard's racing trophies gleaming, and she once tumbled off the dining room table while trying to dust the chandelier above it. I'm sure my dad saw to it that Honeywood curtailed her house work after that.

Dad was as loyal a son as any mother could want. He visited Honey nearly every day, entering through the back porch and whistling loudly to alert hard-of-hearing Honey that he was in the house. (Truth be told, my dad whistled pretty damn loudly wherever he was.)

It was also in the mid-'70s that another house of Honey's houses became an important place in my life.

Broad Avenue, Naples

It was a house of doors. Looking at it from Broad Avenue, Honeywood's cottage in Naples, Florida, looked normal enough, with a screened-in porch spanning its front. But as you walked up the sidewalk, you could see through the screens that there were three doors leading inside from the porch.

On the right, door No. 1 took you into the largest room, with seating set up to view a tabletop TV. On the left, door No. 3 entered into a bedroom. And in the middle, door No. 2 took you into a room of doors—five, to be exact. Four, one on each wall, were traditional doorways, and another one was cut into a paneled wall, providing an almost-secret passage into a bathroom.

The small cottage had four bedrooms, including the grand-union-station room behind door No. 2. Two more bedrooms were on the left side of the cottage, and a fourth was a bed-and-bathroom suite connected to the main room by a short breezeway. The suite must have been added to the original house because a window between the breezeway and the kitchen surely had once been on an exterior wall.

It was Honeywood's parents who bought the Naples property in 1935—for $1,500—and they pieced together a cottage that, while far from fancy, made a grand winter retreat for the family.

Ike and Des had, for years, wintered in Naples, usually with Nat and often with Honey and Howard, who were, by that time, married. This was three years after their son, Jim, had drowned in Kentucky.

Along with the four bedrooms in the main house and addendum, there was a guest house in the back with a bathroom and possibly a kitchenette. By the time I was old enough to remember, the guest house was an uninhabitable jumble of old furniture. It was likely haunted, too (if beach towns even have ghosts).

Mr. Ike died in 1944, and while Honeywood's mother lived another twenty years, she gradually surrendered the Naples cottage to the younger generations. Honey, Howard, and Nat regularly traveled by car or train to Florida, although Howard limited his visits to the months of November and May. He wouldn't go during the winter because, as he'd say, "I am a fisherman, not a tourist."

Honey, too, loved to fish, and she and Howard routinely spent all day fishing off the Naples Pier, located only one block south—and a block and a half west—from their Broad Avenue cottage. She writes in her journal about an epic day—a Thanksgiving Day— when mackerel arrived in large schools. "Howard and I stood on the end of the pier from early morning until dark, bringing up a mackerel on each cast," she wrote in her journal. "Some boys came with gunny sacks and carried them away." When the fish quit biting at sunset, Honey and Howard, exhausted, headed home.

Another of Honey's fishing stories is her trophy-winning catch. She was fishing on the pier without Howard one day, when she struggled to haul in a big fish she had hooked. A stranger had offered to help, but Honey told him, "No, I'd rather lose a fish than to have help." And she eventually reeled it in.

The next day at the same spot—below the bait house, which was situated at the midpoint of the pier—Honey hooked another monster. Unable to make the reel work, Honey had to ask a man nearby if he would help her.

"I thought you'd rather lose a fish than to have help," the man—the same from the day before—said. Though embarrassed, Honey was determined, and together they muscled the fish up to the pier. When Howard arrived later, he took the fish to the bait house and entered it into a contest the municipal pier was running. After returning to Midway, Honeywood received a trophy in the mail, complete with her name, the date, and the weight of the fish. The figure on the top of the trophy was that of a fish being caught…by a man.

As much as Honey loved her Naples home, I did, too. I started going there with my family in 1960, when I was two, and we spent many spring and Christmas breaks at that cottage.

Eventually, I started taking my friends there. From my senior year in high school, 1976, through the mid-'80s, four or five of us would spend a week at Honey's house in Naples every year. Instead of fishing, we focused on drinking—at the beach, in the house, at the bars, and at the house again.

Honeywood had usually headed home to Kentucky before we invaded, but one year, 1979 I think, she was staying longer in Naples. Honey was kind enough—and wise enough—to spend the week several blocks away with a friend.

She was still there when we pulled in from the alley, our car's back end sagging from the eleven cases of beer we had hauled from Kentucky. We were sagging, too, from the eighteen-hour drive that had started after the last final exam was finished.

"I'm on my way out," she said as we lugged our suitcases through the house. "I put some Miller Lite in the fridge for you. I know you boys like your beer." And sure enough, there was a six-pack of cold cans that got us started while we chilled a few of the forty-four six-packs we brought.

The cottage and its furnishings were old enough that the damage caused by four or five boys—and the guests we would invite after the bars closed—was hardly noticeable…to me, anyway. And if Honey noticed, she never said anything.

During that time and afterwards, I don't think Honey was fishing much, but she still enjoyed the beach and floating in the placid gulf on a raft. She was perpetually tan, similar to how she described her father in her journal: "He always had a Florida winter tan and summer farm tan."

Honey died in 1990 at the age of ninety-two. She spent her final years in one of her happy homes, remaining in the big, white house on Winter Street. She spent much of her time in a reclining chair beside a sun-filled window, through which she could watch birds gather at her collection of feeders. She also listened to Cincinnati baseball and Kentucky basketball games on the radio or watched on TV. And she always welcomed a visit from a friend or a member of the family.

Neither Pinkerton Place nor the Naples cottage remain in the family.

At some point in the '80s, Honey was no longer traveling to Naples, and my friends and I had moved our party to the other coast. Honeywood mourned that nobody was enjoying her Naples home anymore, and she sold it.

Letting that crazy little cottage leave the family is my deepest regret in life. Even if I could have worked a deal with Honey, I don't know how I could have looked after the place and paid for utilities and maintenance… but I should have found a way. Our sons would now be fifth-generation Broad Avenue men, and I would be taking Honey's place on the pier, even if I could never match her fishing prowess.

I don't have the same trauma with Pinkerton Place. After Honey passed away, none of us wanted to take on the expense of the grand home, and my dad donated it to Midway College, now Midway University. With donations from supporters, the college undertook a restoration project that no one in our family had the budget for, and Honey's house is now the president's home.

It has come full circle, really. The house was called Pinkerton Place—now Pinkerton-Rouse Place—because a local physician and minister, L.L. Pinkerton, built the original (right-hand) portion of the house around 1845. He ran a boarding school for girls there, and Honeywood, like every resident since, searched unsuccessfully for the names of the girls allegedly etched into window panes.

Dr. Pinkerton had bigger dreams, and in 1847, he teamed with James Ware Parrish, Honeywood's great-grandfather, to found the Kentucky Female Orphan School, which is now Midway University.

I've always thought giving the house to the college was like giving a fine painting to a museum. It's being cared for, plenty of people visit and enjoy it, and I can drop by every so often to admire its beauty…and absorb its memories.

Honey's first home in her memory is Hermosa, followed by the little brown house, Pinkerton Place, and the Naples cottage. From everything she ever said or wrote, she was exceedingly happy in all those homes. That leads me to conclude one thing: It was Honey herself who carried happiness into any home she entered.

The Parrish family's cottage on Broad Avenue in Naples, Florida
Pastel drawing by Sammy Cundiff

Honeywood Parrish Rouse, circa 1916 and age 18

Chapter Five

Honey's Stories

My sister Kay remembers that a highlight of Sunday dinners with our grandparents Howard and Honeywood Rouse were the humorous tales that Howard would tell. But Honeywood was a skilled raconteur, too. The anecdotes below came from two sources: Honey's journal, transcribed by my sister Amy; and Honeywood's own voice, courtesy of a taped interview that Kay conducted.

These are Honeywood's memories of friends and family from her ninety-two years of life in Midway, Kentucky, along with regular visits to the family cottage in Naples, Florida. As she shares amusing stories about the people in her life, Honey also lets us peek into an earlier time, one that seems both passé and pointed… ancient yet anchored.

***

The first school I went to was Miss Maddie Hughes's, just a little country schoolhouse. We had double desks, and she always put a little child with a big one, and the old one was supposed to help teach the younger one to read. George Childers was my deskmate, and he was a crippled boy. He was mostly grown—a big boy—and he carried his leg mostly up and walked with a crutch always. I never thought much about George; he was a nice boy. But in later years, he was running for county jailer, and his opponent came to our house to solicit my vote. He was such a nice-looking man, and I said, "Well yes, what office is it?" He said, "Jailer. I'm running against George Childers." And I said, "Ohhh, I can't vote against George Childers. He taught me to read." The man said, "My goodness. I thought I'd heard every excuse, but I've never heard that before."

***

Eighth-grade arithmetic. I couldn't get it, and neither could my friend Ambrose. She was a bright student, but not very good in arithmetic. But Miss Mary (her mother) and my mother worked on our arithmetic assignments. Ambrose would call me on the phone. "Honey," she'd say, "can Miss Des get number four? Mama got three, but she can't get four."

***

I went to Sayre in Lexington one year, and I had a lovely roommate, Elizabeth Cecil from Danville. Our room was on the second floor, front, and we had a little basket that we'd tie a string to and let it down with our money in it. The night watchman would get our money, go across the street, and get us doughnuts. He'd put the doughnuts in the basket, and we'd pull them up. The night watchman happened to be my Uncle Charlie Rogers, who was retired but had this little job. Back in Midway, my cousin Bird told my sister one day that she had something to get off her chest. She was ashamed that her poor sweet Uncle Charlie was a night watchman. When I heard that, I said, "Well, it's different here. I'm very proud he's a night watchman."

***

Our automobile—a bright red two-seater with the motor in the back—was probably the first one in the neighborhood. People would come for miles to ask Daddy to start up the engine to help their horses get used to them. A car ride with Daddy was the peak of our entertainment. The front seat folded up to make a one-seater out of it. Tollgates were throughout the county, and Daddy would love to make us all get in one seat to go through a tollgate, as it was only fifteen cents for a one-seater but twenty-five cents for a two-seater.

I think he was more interested in fooling the tollgate keeper than he was in saving ten cents!

***

One winter Mama and Daddy took Ambrose and Saxton along with us to Florida. In Georgia we ran into heavy rains. The road was blocked with several cars on either side of this big pond in the road, so we had to spend the night by the roadside. Two nice young men were in the same fix. They had a pup tent, which they set up for Mama, Ambrose, and me. The men all occupied the car seats. They built a big fire, and I read aloud *Gentlemen Prefer Blondes*, which had just come out. The next morning the farmer came down with his mule to pull the cars through the water hole. Daddy wouldn't let him pull us. He said his old Wescott car was very high, and he could drive through. And we did! Daddy said, "That old rascal dug that hole so he could charge two dollars to pull you out." Later on, we came to a part of the road covered with water made red by the Georgia clay. People were sitting around waiting for the water to go down, but Daddy thought he could make it through. He put Saxton up on the hood with a long stick with which he would try to find the road. Saxton would yell out "This way, Pappy," "Not so far," etc. We made it—again. But Mama just barely did… she was petrified.

Ike Parrish in his Westcott, purchased in April 1915

Honeywood Parrish Rouse, circa 1919 and age 21

***

As we were growing up, Ambrose was the belle of Midway, and all the boys fell for her hard. Her father, Dr. Anderson, never took much interest in what we were doing, but there was this one boy from Texas who was visiting Howard's family, and Dr. Anderson didn't want Ambrose to see him. At the time, she was going out with Howard, who was the apple of everybody's eye—all the girls and all the mothers. They'd all love to have Howard, but Ambrose had him. This other boy was determined to go out with Ambrose, though, so here's what we did. Howard had an old car, and he and the boy would come to town. Howard would go get Ambrose, and she'd sit in the front seat. I would sit in the back seat with the other boy. We would go to the Davis's to play tennis, and when we got about as far as the cemetery, we'd stop the car, and Ambrose and I would change places. I think that's where Ambrose started losing Howard and I started winning him.

***

Howard was living in the country with his mother, and after we got married, we went there to live. She was a widow and depended on Howard. He had two brothers still there, Colvin and George. I remember I would think, "Look at the white shirts." Every Monday morning, the washing would be done in big tubs out in the yard. And there'd be twenty-one white shirts washed and hanging on the line—Every. Monday. Morning. Those boys were never allowed to wear the same shirt more than one day. They were the most immaculate family that ever was. So no wonder, when I'd tell people I wanted Mom to come over and see us, they would ask if I was scared to have her visit. I'd say, "No. I just tell her she needs to change clothes before she comes."

***

After Julius was born, Daddy decided that we ought to have a home in town, and Howard said he'd be glad to move. He already made a trip to town every day, so it wasn't any worse to make a trip to the country every day. So Daddy went to this little house he saw that had a for-sale sign, and he asked the woman who lived there how much she wanted for it. "Five thousand dollars," she said. Daddy said, "I'd like to see the garage," so they went and looked at the garage. He didn't want any house that had a garage in the basement or attached to the house, because if the car caught on fire, it would burn the house down. After he looked at the garage, he told the woman he'd take it. She said, "But your wife has not even seen it." And none of us had. Nobody in our family had ever opened the front door. And he said, "Oh, it's not for my wife; it's for my daughter. She likes everything I like."

***

In June 1974, we were in Naples, packing up to come home, and Howard decided to drive up to Gordon's Pass and walk around the point to the channel so he could fish. He had to get permission from a man who ran the Keewaydin boat dock, and Howard told the man he thought he could bring him a snook or two. The man gladly let him walk the private beach and cast for snook. The snook were running in a big way, and without a doubt, Howard had the best fishing he had ever had. Anywhere. He saved all he could carry back to the man, who was overjoyed. Then he came home and told me about it. I insisted we put off going home so he could go back to the pass. This is what he said: "Didn't your mother ever tell you to leave the dance while you were having a good time?" That was his last fishing trip and his last summer. He died in September 1974. But wasn't that a fairy-tale ending for a fisherman?

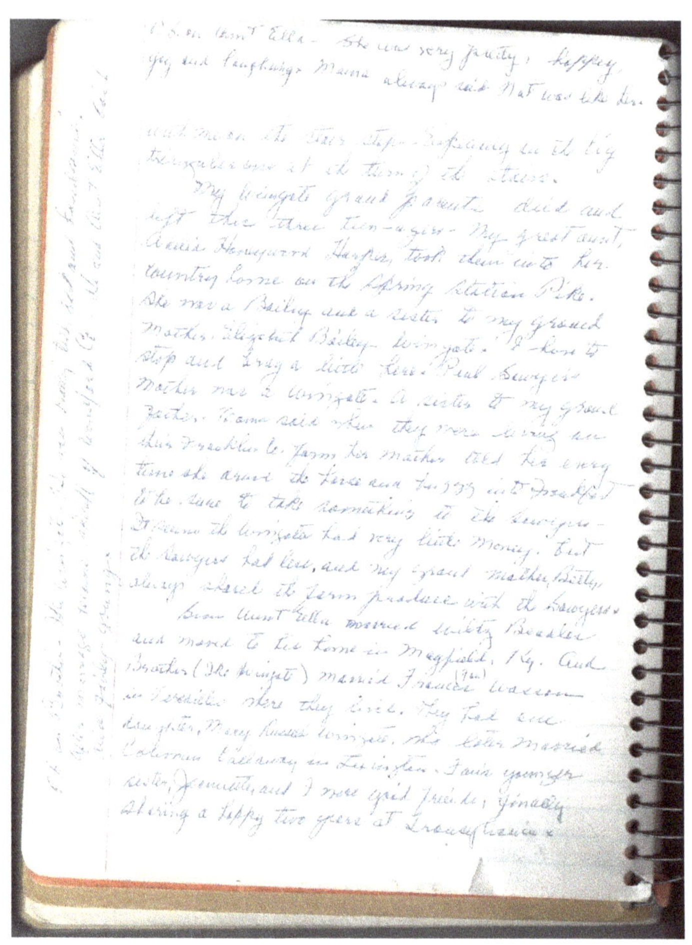

A page from Honeywood's handwritten journal; it includes the origin of her unique name and a reference to the family of her cousin, noted painter Paul Sawyier.

Howard and Honeywood, circa 1970

A young Ike Rouse, age 7, dancing with a family dog during a summer up home

Chapter Six

A Boy Up Home

My father, Ike, was a town kid. He lived with Honeywood and Howard on Winter Street, Midway's main drag, but he spent plenty of time "up home" with his Parrish grandparents and Aunt Nat. And after he married my mom, Jean, they extended the driveway, cleared a spot in the apple orchard, and built a house near Hermosa.

In a 2007 interview with my sister Amy, Dad recalls his days as a boy at Hermosa in the 1930s and '40s. The Parrish residence sat on ten acres—not a full-fledged farm, but a productive ecosystem for family, friends, and visitors. His comments below were transcribed by Amy and then edited for clarity…but you get the picture.

***

The Parrish family raised practically everything they ate, buying only flour, honey, white sugar, salt, and pepper. Mama Des ran the operation. They had a half-acre garden in two parts, with a grape trellis down the middle. There were no machines back then, and to work the garden was mainly a matter of strength and awkwardness. Where our house is was an apple orchard, and there were a couple of pear trees behind what's now Ouita and Chris's house. There were cherry trees, but I don't think they ever had peaches.

They put up all kinds of vegetables in jars—green beans, tomatoes, and corn…a ton of corn. Most of the food they put up was stored in the basement of the house—massive amounts. They ran practically a restaurant over there. My grandfather was always "come on up and eat with us," and my grandmother just stayed ready. She never knew how many would be there for dinner.

***

The outbuildings included two chicken houses, one for the baby chicks and one for the laying hens; a pigeon house; an icehouse; and quarters for their help. The one building I was unsure of was a smokehouse for hams. There was something else there, but I don't remember. My Uncle Jim had a Model T Ford, and he used it for a garage. Then there was the buggy house, and they added a gas heater in there when they got cars.

The icehouse was located underneath the shop, which was filled with tools and a work bench. When the electric refrigerator came and they quit cutting ice, that's when they converted the icehouse into a mushroom cellar. My main summer job was to haul the chicken manure to the mushroom cellar. I have no idea why…I don't believe they ever used that many mushrooms.

***

There was a barn for the milk cows, and they always had two milk cows: one that was fresh and one that was waiting to be fresh.

They used to keep the farm mules in that same barn. Every workday, the men from the farm would walk in and get their mules, ride them back to the farm, work them all day, ride them back to the barn, and then finally walk back home. This was a four-mile round trip each day for the work hands, as the farm was a mile away from the barn, and their house on the farm was a mile from the farm gate.

***

In the main house, I remember it was heated with a gas furnace and hot-water radiators. They also had gas lights in the house.

***

When I think about eating up home, I remember there was always lots of food, and Mama Des supervised all the cooking. All meals were served in the main dining room, except in summertime, when we'd eat on the side porch. There was a fold-down table out there that stayed up on the wall when not in use.

Back then, "dinner" was the noontime meal and "supper" was the evening meal. The table was set for all meals: white linen tablecloth and napkins, silverware, and China. No wine was served with meals. Drinks were served beforehand in another part of the house.

***

After supper—during the summer months, anyway—the family would often retire to the porch. They'd listen to the radio, choosing between the two or three nothing stations available back then, and they'd listen to shows like "Amos and Andy."

Also during the summer months, lots of visitors came. Friends and family would come for a few days…that turned into weeks. My grandparents made sure the dining room table would have all the leaves put in, practically filling the room.

At the end of every meal, Ike Parrish insisted that each serving dish be full—refilled in the kitchen and passed again to guests. He wasn't being wasteful; he just didn't want anyone to go away hungry.

***

Years later, Amy went to Dad for more insights into the family home. Amy and Ouita Michel (the current-day owner of the house, The Holly Hill Inn) had hired a ghost hunter to assess the property for paranormal energy and potential hauntings. I won't go into their findings here—that's their book to write—other than Amy's conversation with Dad.

The ghost hunters had identified a large maple tree by the side entrance as a spot where something "extreme" happened—perhaps a horrible accident or worse: a murder or hanging. When asked about the maple, Dad's demeanor indeed reflected tragedy. He grew serious and silent. Eventually, he told the sordid tale.

"The tree that's there is not the original maple," he said. "What we see today grew from the stump of a locust tree. And that old locust tree held secrets."

Amy, still a little disappointed that the ghost hunt had not revealed any detailed hauntings, was on the edge of her seat when Dad finished the story.

"When I was up home with my grandparents during the summer, there were days when I would go swimming without getting permission from my mother. It was on those days…and in that old maple…that I would stash my wet bathing suit so my mother wouldn't know I'd gone swimming."

Photos of Ike Rouse at Hermosa, circa 1933. Top: on hand for construction of a large windmill. Bottom: leaning against the "bathing suit tree" (with the shop in the background at right)

Holly Hill Inn hostess Jackie Anthony greets diners on a summer evening.

Chapter Seven

Hermosa Today
The Holly Hill Inn

The storm door doesn't quite latch.

I recall noticing it when my dad and I met with Ouita and Chris Michel in 2000 to talk about selling the Holly Hill Inn to them. I had noticed it over the previous twenty years, when Rex and Rose Lyons ran the inn and I was there for dinners, parties, and wedding receptions, including Mary Beth's and mine.

And look, maybe the storm door had never latched properly. Maybe it didn't fully close back when my great-aunt Nat lived there. Up until her death in 1970, I was in that house all the time—not just for family dinners but also for everyday visits I'd make as a child to see what Nat and her cook, Siretha, were up to. We lived just a hundred yards away, and I always used the side porch door, closest to our house. So maybe the front door was faulty and maybe it wasn't. I never used it to know.

On this night, though, I walk in through the front door.

I am here at Hermosa with a purpose. Because I have been writing about the house and my Parrish forebears who lived there three generations ago, I need to complete the circle. To really see what the house as it is today. To understand what Hermosa has become since my family sold it nearly a quarter century ago.

Of course, I've been to the Holly Hill Inn many times since the Michels bought it—for family gatherings, intimate anniversary dinners, outings with friends, and even political rallies. But I've always come as a guest.

Tonight, though, I'm part of the house. I sit in the front hall, tucked into a corner that was once anchored by Nat's grand piano, ordered from Cincinnati when her musical talent became evident in the early 1900s. The piano is now at our house—mostly unplayed yet still loaded with Nat's notes.

Jackie Anthony is the hostess on this fine April evening, welcoming patrons and showing them to the tables they reserved—maybe a month ago and maybe this morning. There are tables of varying sizes in each of the three downstairs rooms used for seatings, two parlors and the dining room. One of the upstairs rooms is set for a group of eight, and on the porch, there's one group and one solo diner.

"No turns tonight," Jackie says to a co-worker. That means on this Thursday, every table will be used only once. She tells me that on some nights, they'll book a table at 5:30 or six and again at eight. She estimates two hours for a party to finish; longer for a large group and quicker for a two-top. Even more guests are slated for Saturday night, when the weather will turn too cold for outdoor dining, so the staff will turn a few tables.

The servers move quickly but carefully, gliding out of each other's way. One walks with an empty plate from the second course, and another is delivering a just-mixed cocktail. Most of the waitstaff are seasoned professionals and have been with Ouita for years. I know Jackie's father and his brothers from my growing-up days in Midway.

***

Dinner here is not cheap. The five-course prix fixe meal costs seventy dollars, and the alcohol tab can mount quickly. But it's an experience. I've always thought the cost of a meal here goes well beyond the food and drink. I'm also renting space for a while, and a parade of friendly people keep refilling my plate and my glass.

This restaurant is well known locally, and beyond the Bluegrass, too. The Holly Hill Inn, Ouita, or both have been covered by *The New York Times*, *Garden & Gun*, *Southern Living*, CBS, and other national media outlets. Each year, the inn's chairs are filled by guests from every state, and Ouita has personally greeted diners from more than two dozen countries. It doesn't stop here, either: The Holly Hill Inn is Chef Ouita's flagship restaurant in a fleet of six other Central Kentucky dining spots.

My only contribution to Ouita's success is helping to get her here twenty-plus years ago, but I nevertheless feel pride in her success. And I've always felt good about selling off the family home to Ouita and Chris.

Now I leave my front hall perch and move to what used to be the side porch; it's now the bar and a staging area for servers. They don't walk silently through this area. It has a bouncy floor that squeaks. I worry for a second about how long these old boards can last, but then I settle in and enjoy the music they make.

From the side porch is a staircase that leads to another porch upstairs, one that was used by Nat and her siblings, Honeywood and Jim, as a sleeping space on hot summer nights. It was from there that they watched the great distillery fire in downtown Midway; my grandmother Honeywood described the calamitous night in her journal. The year was 1908, and Honey was ten.

As I look toward town tonight, I can't imagine how Honey could see through all the trees; in summer they would surely be leafed out. But then I decide that most of the trees I see this evening were planted when houses were built in Northridge subdivision, adjacent to the inn's property. Back in 1908—and throughout my young days, too—it was just an empty field with no trees to block the view of bourbon ablaze.

Today that porch is used to store restaurant supplies, everything from glass mugs and stirring straws to binder clips and rolls of receipt paper.

Nat's old bedroom, located over the dining room and just off the upstairs porch, is now the wine, um, cellar. Next to it, over the kitchen, is her brother Jim's old room. I'm not sure if I want to go in. That's where we found that lock of auburn hair in a little box in a desk drawer fifty years ago.

I do go in Jim's room, entering from the other end of the porch. I find no ghosts or curls of hair, though, just more restaurant stuff.

***

I go back downstairs to visit the heart of the business—the kitchen. As a child, when I would wander over from next door, the kitchen was my first stop. Nat might be in there making breakfast, and I'd grab a piece of bacon. Even better, Siretha might be icing a cake, and I'd clean out the pan with a spoon. The place sure seemed roomy enough back then.

Not so tonight. The restaurant-grade stove and two warming ovens take up a lot of space. And even though the old kitchen sink is gone, with dishwashing activities relocated to a small back porch, it's still tight quarters. There are four chefs and a dishwasher here, and they work efficiently—focused but friendly. Music is playing, and one chef hums along while another bounces silently to the beat.

Servers drop in to explain special requests—additions or deletions—and one chef is the expediter, labeled by a colleague as "the conductor of the orchestra." Working from printed order slips and an iPad mounted on the wall, she calls out what's needed: "Two lamb, two medium-rare duck, three fish!" Then, to another chef: "Three salads and two soups."

It makes me think of the 1978 Saturday Night Live skit set at The Olympia Restaurant, with Dan Aykroyd at the grill and John Belushi and Lorraine Newman calling out orders of the only entrée on the menu: chee-burger, chee-burger, chee-burger. It's like that at the Holly Hill Inn kitchen, but times ten…maybe times fifty.

A little skillet with red snapper sizzles on the flames from the gas stove, and next to it, a fry pan is filled with pasta that gets tossed and turned. There are timers and buzzers going off sporadically. Standing away from the stove, one chef prepares desserts, plating a flourless dark chocolate torte with a scoop of caramel ice cream and topping them with other sweet fineries.

I wouldn't call that kitchen chaotic, but man, the energy is exhilarating.

I would definitely call it warm. On this April evening at 7:30, the temperature in the kitchen is 103 degrees. I don't want to think about July…but I'll say this, when I'm there with my family for Thanksgiving in July, I'll sure be thinking about the kitchen crew. I always try to be generous with my tips so that servers feel appreciated—more so since the pandemic. I'll take it a step further and tip the kitchen, too.

***

By 7:45, I'm back in the front hall. Every diner who's coming tonight has been seated and served something: a drink, an amuse-bouche, a salad, or maybe dessert already. Jackie's job is nearly done, and she prepares to go home. She tells me about a recent first-time customer who pulled her aside and said, "Congratulations."

He told Jackie that, to a person, the staff had been so nice...so genuine. "You've made me feel at home."

That's the whole idea, of course. And it's forever a home, Hermosa, now the Holly Hill Inn. The floor might squeak, the storm door might hang, and the memories of Jim Parrish are long gone. Even a stranger feels at home here...as do I.

Chef Ouita Michel, 2022

MIDW

Chapter Eight

My Midway

I have never lived in Midway. That might come as a shock to people who I've met outside of Midway, because I have long been an unabashed champion of my hometown…well, my home area.

I must mention Midway a lot. I've mostly worked at jobs in Lexington, and more than one colleague has referred to me as the "mayor of Midway" (as if Midway is too small to have an actual mayor). Other acquaintances have said I must serve on the Midway Chamber of Commerce (which doesn't really exist). And when I made a whimsical pitch to invite the Toronto Blue Jays to Midway for their

2020 season—when COVID restricted travel to and from Canada—my love for Midway got media attention on both sides of the border.

It's right there in black and white, too. In my collection of Midway-based short stories, *Christmas in the Bluegrass*, here's my dedication:

> *To Midway, the finest town a boy could ever be born in, born to, and born of.*

It's all true, too. Midway is that awesome. Except I don't really live there. I've never resided inside the city limits. So what's my deal? Why do I latch on to this tiny town—population 1,742—as if my identity depends on it?

I don't know, but I'm going to figure it out. By the time I finish writing this, you—and I—will discover the answer.

My dad, Ike, lived in Midway. He grew up on Winter Street, the only surviving child of Honeywood and Howard Rouse. When he married Jean Coleman, my mom, in the mid-'50s, they built a house on North Winter Street behind what's now the Holly Hill Inn. Today's inn was yesterday's Hermosa, the childhood home of Honeywood, who was the oldest of three Parrish children.

I grew up in that house near Hermosa, just a short distance from the city limits. Empty fields sat next to us, and I could sled the hills, shoot a BB gun, and putter around on a minibike. We weren't in the country—the rooftops of Midway were only a quarter-mile away—but we weren't in town, either. I didn't walk down the block to see my friends; either they arrived by car or I was driven to them.

The Friday nights when my sisters and I spent the night with Honey and Howard were a thrill, because I was in Midway proper, with houses and people and yards cheek-to-cheek. If the weather was tolerable, there'd be a dozen or more neighborhood kids who would gather outside to play flashlight tag and other games. As it got dark, they would, one by one, respond to various parental bells, whistles, or hollers that meant it was time to come inside.

It was like these people, whose homes were a short distance from my home, had a whole different way of living.

Truth be told, I felt like an outsider…sort of like the out-of-towner Dill Harris hanging around Scout and Jem and scoping out Boo Radley. It's not that the neighborhood kids didn't welcome me; they did, and we were friends. But I *felt* Dill-like (while not being, I hope, quite so dorky.)

When I got a little older, I also got more invested in the town of Midway. Part of that came from playing on the Midway Elementary basketball team in the fourth through sixth grades. I was proud to wear "Midway" across my chest and Converse All-Stars on my feet.

Our school building had once housed grades one through twelve. Both my dad and grandfather went to Midway High there. That little school won the state basketball championship in 1937, beating out big-city teams as well as other small-town dreamers. Dad said that after Midway took the state title, everybody in town seemed to hold their head a little higher and walk with more pep in each step.

I started at power forward for the Midway Blue Jays in '66 and '67. Now, nobody ever said I played that position; neither Coach Haynes nor any of my teammates spoke of me as a power forward. I was one of the taller kids, though, and somebody once told me I was almost a good rebounder, so that's the position I claim. I sure as hell wasn't the shooting forward, as I was mostly afraid I'd miss.

Another factor that increased my Midway identity was my bicycle. It was a Schwinn or a Raleigh, I don't remember. What I remember for sure is that it wasn't a Stingray, with the chopper handlebars, banana seat, stainless steel stick shift, and slick back tire. I had a sensible road bike. But it had three speeds and front handbrakes that could, potentially, flip a rider over the sensible handlebars if squeezed too hard. Not exactly badass, but slightly dangerous, at least.

And for sure, I was lucky to have a bike at all; I know that now. I sort of knew it then, though I often pity-partied about not having a cooler bike.

But with my sensible bike, I could routinely ride to Midway, flying down Cogartown Hill and laboring up Town Hill. It allowed me to be more of a regular Midway kid. I could pedal from hot spot to hot spot: Midway Drug, Kirk's Grocery, and the sandlot baseball field beside the Presbyterian Church. Or I could park my bike in Honey and Howard's garage and then hang out on the streets of Midway. (Note: If anybody ever called them the mean streets of Midway, they must've meant the streets were average, not dangerous.)

Spending more time in Midway allowed me to flex my social muscles, and I'd look for excuses to be in town. When I started junior high school and rode the bus from Versailles, I would get off at Midway Elementary so I could walk to the doctor's office to get my weekly shot for asthma. (Not even Dill Harris did that, I bet). More often than not, I would get caught up playing backyard football or trading baseball cards and "miss" getting to the doctor's office before it closed. (They would lock the door at four.) So, darn it all, I'd have to get off the bus in town the next day, too.

Once my friends and I got our driver's licenses and started cruising nearby Versailles, my Midway time diminished some, but not altogether. I stayed grounded in Midway for three reasons: a girl, a ball field, and a youth group.

In the summer of '72 I started dating a girl who lived right next door to Honey and Howard, and we were off and on for the next nine years. (Eventually she told me she was moving away from Midway to enhance her job prospects, and I have always chosen to believe it was her career—and not me—that led her to leave town.) I can't tell you how many hours we spent on the swing of her front porch while the world drove by on Winter Street.

During the summer, we would often walk down the street to the ball field in a bottom beside Midway Elementary. That's where the action was. It's where the men of Midway and the surrounding area played softball, and the competition in both the farm league and the church league was as keen as a Yankees–Red Sox series in September. More remarkable than the play was the racial integration. Unlike in Midway's neighborhoods or churches, Black and White folks congregated together at the ball field like it was a normal thing. And so it became a normal thing.

One other activity that gave me a powerful Midway affiliation was the Midway Christian Church youth group. We had a minister, Bill McDonald, who brought a fresh style of ecclesiastic leadership to Midway, and teenagers from his church and others (including my sister Amy and me, who bolted from the Presbyterian Church) formed a tight-knit group that learned and loved and traveled together. When we went to district retreats or church camp, everybody knew that Midway Christian was in the house. We were a small-town, white-bread gang, and it was life-changing.

All these things—Blue Jays basketball, Kirk's Grocery, allergy shots, a church gang, and a softball field—anchored me in Midway. That town/that name/those streets/those people…teamed up to shape me. To teach me. To make me who I am today.

What I am not today is a famous author. I will never be a big-time scribbler because, with my remarkably happy childhood, I never lived the pain that powers the poignant truths that successful writers wring from their tortured souls. (And yes, I'm setting aside the probability that I also lack the skill to shoot to the top of the best-seller lists.)

For the record, my growing-up days weren't perfect. My athletic career peaked in the fifth grade, my academic prowess fell off when I reached junior high, and pretty girls routinely broke my heart.

But my growing-up days were damn near idyllic. I was surrounded by a stable, loving family as well as stable—and unstable—friends. I grew up in a home with books and newspapers and was able to travel often. And I always returned to a safe place: my home and my hometown.

I don't know what led my great–great–great–great–great–grandfather and grandmother, James and Tabitha Parrish, to land in this place, but their 1781 journey from Virginia ended here. And if Midway—or, at least, the Greater Midway Area—were a genetic trait, I sure inherited it.

My grandfather Howard was the mayor of Midway for many years, but I did not inherit that title. When an out-of-town friend tries to label me mayor of Midway, I disavow it, often pointing out that I'm ineligible to run. What I don't say, but should, is that there is a very real mayor, and she and her predecessors—and scores of council members and other leaders—are doing the day-to-day work of making Midway a fantastic little town. I'm merely cheering from the stands.

I actually lived in Lexington for a dozen or so years following college. Living first with several buddies and then marrying and staying in the big city, I liked being close to restaurants and bars and stores. But after Mary Beth and I had our first child, we decided that Midway offered a better environment for raising a family. And so we raised our two boys in my hometown…a mile outside the city limits, you know.

Several years ago, I was in the middle of a telephone survey, and the question was, "What makes the place you live unique?"

It stumped me. For every answer that came to mind, I envisioned people in a hundred other places—ten thousand other places—saying the same thing: oh, the beautiful surroundings, the small-town welcome, the special people...

I couldn't answer honestly with any of those descriptions because they simply weren't unique. Everything Midway has—natural beauty, friendly vibe, great food, and nice neighbors—could also be claimed by residents of most any small town.

But here's the thing: This is *my* small town. It's unique to *me*. There are dusty ball fields and youth group movie nights and hand-holding girlfriends in every tiny town in America—big cities, too. But I got all those things from my Midway...and nowhere else.

I don't live in Midway, but by God, Midway sure lives in me.

Appendix

The Parrish Family of Hermosa

Isaac Williams Parrish
Purchased Hermosa 1903
1868–1944 (76 years)

Desdemona Wingate Parrish
Purchased Hermosa 1903
1874–1964 (90 years)

Elizabeth Honeywood Parrish Rouse
Grew up in Hermosa
1898–1990 (92 years)

Katherine "Nat" Wingate Parrish
Grew up in Hermosa
1902–1970 (68 years)

James Ware Parrish III
Grew up in Hermosa
1905–1932 (27 years)

Julius Howard Rouse
Honeywood's husband
1896–1974 (78 years)

Isaac Parrish Rouse
Honeywood's son
1926–2011 (84 years)

Jean Taylor Coleman Rouse
Isaac's wife
1925–1991 (66 years)

Kay Coleman Rouse Lark
Grew up next door to Hermosa
Husband, Andy; daughter, Terry

Amy Parrish Rouse Perry
Grew up next door to Hermosa
Husband, Mike; daughters Lauren and Liz

Robert Wingate Rouse
Grew up next door to Hermosa
Wife, Mary Beth; sons Steele and Clay